Although this book contains cartoons that I hope will put a smile on its reader's f
forgotten that the underlying theme and objective is a serious one. The main enc
eradicate this continuing 21st century scourge: Monarchy, from Britain and coun
unfortunate enough to be chained and subjugated by it. This book is dedicated to parents and children throughout the world who still have to endure this or any other form of absolute rule. Their resolve must be to ensure that all people are free from the constraints of servility and the class divisive and deferential imposition of 'subject' and be liberated into the real, not pseudo world of true CITIZENSHIP. Indeed the February 2004 display of citizenship employed by the British government and the inclusion of a Princely mediocrity was an embarrassing attempt at real democracy. Britain needs to emulate the far superior democracies of France and Germany and legislate for a Citizen's charter where allegiance does not include the absurd declaration of loyalty to an un-elected Head-of-State; an act that is the very anthithesis of democracy. Shamefully, it is a preposterous deception practised on the people of this nation by a parliamentary institution that purports to be the Mother-of-all-Parliaments?

Parents and children: your charge is to eliminate inequality, and promote justice in Britain and throughout the rest of the deprived world, where autocratic Monarchy exists. Monarchy is a tyranny that denies people their natural choice of Citizenship and so much more. Always carry this thought in your head, "in a true democracy no person should ever be above the law of the land and able to exert enormous power in perpetuity". An injustice that Britain has to endure, but which we should all strive and fight to banish from Britain's class ridden society without delay. *William Gladys.*

Copyright. Held equally May 2003, between William Gladys and Andy Mac. The rights of both are identified as joint authors of this work: *Monarchy – Politics of Tyranny and Denial*. This is asserted in accordance with section 77 of the Copyright, Design and Patents Act 1988. The artwork in this publication was commissioned by William Gladys from Andy Mac, although the views and opinions expressed herein, textually or graphically, are not necessarily those held by the artist. email: williamgladys@tiscali.co.uk

Published 2004 by Derek Books, Carmarthenshire, Cymru, UK.   Email: derekbooks@hotmail.com

All rights reserved. No part of this publication may be reproduced, stored in a retrieval system, or transmitted, in any form or by any means, electronic, mechanical, photocopying, recording or otherwise, without the prior permission of the publishers. This book is sold subject to the condition that it shall not, by way of trade or otherwise, be lent, resold, hired out or otherwise circulated without the publisher's prior consent in any form of binding or cover other than that in which it is published and without a similar condition including this condition being imposed on the subsequent purchaser.

ISBN 0-9547575-0-5

QUEEN'S ASTONISHING PROCLAMATION!

A recent pronouncement by the Queen at the Welsh Assembly was an admirable advertisement for abolition of Monarchy. It is astounding to think that if it was written by her or a close advisor that neither of them was aware of its Anti-Monarchical significance!

"Democratic election is the fundamental means by which every elector can participate in the business of government and … we must encourage all our people to exercise their democratic rights."

Well that's rich and beggars' belief coming from an **unelected** Head-of-State. What impudence, hypocrisy, and cheek!! Does she include herself and relations in this electoral category, or do they consider themselves something other than people? There was no mention of people's right to citizenship. Neither was there an apology or denunciation of our continuing role as demeaning, discreditable, subservient subjects. Nor indeed any challenging questions from the media or protest from a timid, boring and (pre-selected) acquiescent audience!! Some Anti-Monarchists declare they have no wish to affront the Queen however. They shouldn't have any misgivings about that! From a contradictory standpoint there are those who consider her presence over decades has been an unrelenting affront to the people of this nation. It is time for her and Monarchy to remove the shackles of tyranny and denial and go.

Ze Schrecklich Deceit

"I am ze engleesh from ze top of ze head to ze tip of ze toe"! In the TV drama *The Lost Prince*, Queen Mary Von Teck our present Queen's grandmother was portrayed as speaking with a posh English accent. According to the information I have been given this was not true, she spoke with a pronounced guttural accent. This is hardly surprising since her dynasty descended from recent German origins. This suggests that yet again an individual or group anxious to 'rearrange' the facts has been instrumental in distorting the truth to protect the royal image.

In 1917 Britain was at war with Germany and ruled by a German Monarch. Almost overnight any trace of Saxe-Coburg-Gotha, Hesse, Battenberg and Schleswig-Holstein, was magically removed from the lists and replaced with Windsor. This disreputable Monarch was prepared to sacrifice his heritage and betray his ancestry in order to appease and deceive the British people so that his family could continue to wallow in the power and luxury of the British throne! I am not racist, I have many German friends. However, each and every one of them is appalled and dismayed by such blatant treachery. Regrettably the British press to their discredit was party to this terrible or in German, Schrecklich deceit, which continues to the present day. The drawing of Mary Von Teck emphasizes the Germanic roots, spiked hat, jackboots, rigid inflexible manner, and so on. The outer skin of our reigning dynasty may have changed;
New name, new accent, new image, sophisticated marketing, but has the old Germanic inner core changed also?

Blair's Ear

A large majority of voters in England and Wales want a total ban on the barbaric 'sport' of fox hunting. The Prime Minister and the Minister for Rural Affairs were indecisive. Now it seems, thankfully, they will NOT renege on their manifesto promise. However, it is clear from press reports that voters supportive of a total ban may be disregarded by the House of Lords while the rural rich and royals are listened to. This would be a scandalous and prejudiced decision by **Her Majesty's** second chamber. These two words are significant because it is clear that the government would **NOT** in this case belong to the people! If the latter were true, there is little doubt that the Parliament Act would be implemented and the act placed on the statute books without hindrance. While Blair or any future Prime Minister continues weekly visits to Buckingham Palace to discuss politics with our unelected Head-of-State however, does anyone seriously believe that some 'matters' are not rearranged? Will the quaintly named House of Lords be acting impartially? Is it inconceivable that Prince Charles is **not** given special consideration over issues that he feels strongly about? (See cartoon about green ink letters). Minutes of these meetings are **NOT** available for the taxpaying people of Britain to inspect. The tête-à-têtes with the Queen may be lawful, but are morally indefensible. It is an outrageous rebuff to the legitimate electorate, and should be rectified as soon as possible.

This point is raised in the cartoon where royals are shown exerting their power over Blair, a continuation of the weekly audience perhaps? Under the well heeled Prince Charles, dominant in his hand made hunting boots, the anti-hunt majority is downtrodden and deemed unworthy of consideration. The will of the people may still be thwarted however if the Lords' give their support to this small but powerful and immensely wealthy minority. This would be a mockery of justice. The people's majority would be overridden to benefit those who own **most of our nation's heritage: our land. Let us hope that Blair's ear will not be tweaked enough for him to renege against the will of the people.**

Princess 'Wonderful Mind'

Princess Margaret started life with enormous advantages but chose to abuse them: a large proportion of it spent on frivolity, extravagance, self-indulgence, booze, sex and luxury sun-drenched island living. This brand of lifestyle was funded by the British taxpayer and should not have been tolerated. What makes the situation worse however, is that she allegedly encouraged sycophancy and undignified servility in the 'commoners' who were present to pamper to her every whim. For those engaged in such soul destroying deference, it is essential that it is not acceded to; otherwise it can soon degenerate into an interminable downward spiral of deceit, delusion and destruction of self belief.

The idea for this cartoon came from an accumulation of press snippets over the years, as well as a recent unchallenged discussion on the radio. A Monarchist assured us that "Princess Margaret had a wonderful, wonderful mind". The cartoon aims to reject that statement, and bring some sense into the discussion. Numerous degrees are shown, but in reality as far as we are aware she did not possess one, nor did she leave us any writing to learn from and advance our intellect.

So much for this "wonderful, wonderful mind"

Resting between her legs and overweight body we see a copy of The Daily Mail.

Power but Not the Glory

THE ROYALS by Kitty Kelley, and published in the U.S.A., could be considered the most damning publication ever written about the royals in the last decade. It is not freely available in Britain. To obtain a copy is difficult. Authorities in Britain do their utmost NOT to get involved. By searching the web however, a bookseller in England who believed ardently in freedom-of-speech let me have a copy. Contacts with publishers, public libraries and the news media proved negative. In a lot of cases I sensed a vibrant undercurrent of fear! If only a few of the allegations are true, the publication is dynamite as far as this anachronistic institution and its parasitic hangers on are concerned. Many of the statements purportedly come from more than one source, and could be verified, yet vital and important public information is denied inspection by the British people? Maybe libel laws and freedom-of-speech in Britain need an urgent and thorough overhaul. Until that day arrives democratic accountability in this country of ours is a non-starter.

The illustration makes it clear that publishers, libraries and a large part of the media have decided to evade the issue hence the three sheep illustrated. In tandem with this conscious decision is the British bulldog, symbolising the media here. Although anxious to please and enlighten the British people, he is held in check by a leash controlled by the power and influence of Monarchy.

If the media is not prepared to activate their inalienable moral right to publish vital issues of momentous importance to the British population and in the interest of freedom-of-speech and freedom of information, why bother to carry insurance in the first place?

As You Like It!

A number of distasteful facts were revealed at the trial of royal butler Paul Burrell. Detailed disclosure of Prince Charles's book throwing assault on his butler for example. It was a disgraceful act and is deplored by everyone. Now that the facts are in the open however, what action will the police authority concerned be taking? In similar circumstances, an employee on the receiving end of this type of violent behaviour would have resorted to the law or other organisations for redress. Is there one law for royals, and another for the rest of us? Does this strengthen the case for eliminating the rules of confidentiality so rigorously applied to the rather odd people who work for royals and in royal establishments? Is the book assault the tip of the iceberg; is there more that should be exposed for public scrutiny in the interest of justice? No balanced individual could possibly condone such deplorable action in a place of employment or anywhere for that matter. Public reaction was condemnatory, but the press response was muted in relation to the severity of the act. We can all envisage the headlines if a high profile 'celebrity' or business executive had been guilty of an identical act of aggression:

Violent Boss! This Monster <u>Must</u> Resign Now!

This cartoon encapsulates the outrage of the people as they vent their fury on behalf of the rest of us. The main thrust of the title is centred on Shakespeare's *As You Like It*. Saying see how **you** like having an object hurled at you. It also reminds us of his interest in Shakespeare's works and his purported belief that the majority of inherent themes in them can be used as a prop or justification for Monarchy. The opposite is often the case however once the texts have been subjected to detailed analysis. It depends so much on each individual's political perspective and starting point. It is alarming to think that this person is now politically involved in forming our educational curriculum! Meetings with members of parliament engaged in educational matters confirm this. Standing behind the stocks a British policeman appropriately turns a blind eye to the situation? Silent approval that this pampered prince is, in cartoon form at least reaping what he has sown and so justly deserves!

Goodness Gracious How Ungracious!

At the royal butler Paul Burrell's trial it was revealed that he had to stand for three hours while being interrogated by the Queen. No doubt this woman had the freedom to roam while her 'commoner' subject had to endure disgraceful indignity and discomfort. His revelations exposed the distasteful, intolerable side of working for royals and Monarchy. A most ungracious and ignoble act ma'am, and one of which you should be ashamed. He mentioned her 'soliloquy', the harping on about "…the dark forces out there that one should be wary of…" This is not verbatim, but the gist of what was allegedly espoused with such dark foreboding… Well Mr. Burrell, now you know, there are more things in heaven and earth, than are dreamt of in your philosophy. But come, worry not how odd and strange she sounds!! Whatever the consequences of such a comic/tragic event, it raises urgent questions about rights of employment in royal establishments. In the real world employers are governed by legislation and human rights considerations, where abuse of this significance would not be tolerated. Unions, if retained, would have sought recompense of some kind, and the media would not have shied away from forthright criticism. Royals must conform to rules and regulations that other employers have to abide by, and their outmoded rules of confidentiality be drastically reformed in favour of the people. Royal employees should rightfully campaign for a written contract of employment. Pay slips or salary statements should be made available for scrutiny if the employee gives his or her permission. There should be no recrimination whatsoever if this action was resorted to. Those who work for the royals should not consider themselves special or privileged, but **put upon and rather odd!** They have a moral justification to reveal 'secrets' of a deplorable and damaging nature. High technology is freely available. Employees should consider extra 'insurance' for their own protection and think about installing detection devices for verification of irrefutable truth if needed later. Incidentally, WHERE ARE THE UNIONS HIDING? YOUR HELP IS URGENTLY SOUGHT.

In the cartoon her wretched butler is shown in great discomfort. Knees locked together trying to retain the flow of urine from his overstretched bladder. The sand timer records his agony of three hours. Behind his back a silver tray is held in check! His stance portrays the accumulative effect of years of **deference and kowtowing** but evaporating by the second. Perhaps on the verge of rightly losing his temper and clouting this **ungracious woman** about the head, the interrogation comes to an end!

Royal Super Hype

To accept the pretentious title **'The Queen Mother'** highlights her exaggerated self importance. An attitude regrettably condoned by most of the media, and a morally bad example to set before our children. Had Nelson Mandela adopted a similar high blown title for his own mother i.e. **'The President Mother'**, the British media would have had a hey-day. Removing the apostrophe is grammatically bad, but also the worst form of affectation. Use of this dreadful title was not an irrelevance, as suggested by some. Far from it. One of its aims was to condition people to accept a deferential and subservient role in British society relevant to the royals, while elevating the Queen's mother to an elitist position that 'commoners' could never aspire to. A dangerous and contentious issue for our children and important for them to resolve **sooner** rather than later. Whatever happened to free speech, free expression and the strength of British character and independence of mind of those prepared to publicly stand against the nonsense of anachronistic convention and reject over-hyped protocol? As a media correspondent was heard to say at the time of the funeral:

"No arse licking now"!!

But in reality the majority did just that and timidly doffed their caps to royalty! In the cartoon the Queen's mother has been placed in a transcendent pose, with halo and matching angel wings. This stance replicates the establishment and Media's resolve to induce 'mass' adulation in the public domain. They were successful up to a point, transforming a royal mediocrity into a temporary myth of saintliness. The hype surrounding her demise was deplorable, insulting and deceitful. This was confirmed by rabid condemnation of a TV presenter who had the audacity to wear a maroon tie!! Perhaps like a great number of people in Britain, he was not prepared to toe the establishment line, and be goaded into insincere solemnity for the sake of an anachronistic institution and its overbearing members.

Royal fall from Hype

When the Queen's mother died, the media coverage was viewed with disbelief by millions of people. At the time it seemed as if it would never end the coverage and time allocated to it being viewed as out of proportion to its importance. News of national and world shattering significance was sidelined. This was the spur and one of the reasons for this cartoon.

In a previous cartoon the over-hype surrounding her demise was highlighted in The Daily Trivia. In this one she appears in The Daily Significance, where she is brought back to reality. Life affecting issues like interest rates, Bin Laden and terrorism occupy most of the pages. In the bottom right hand corner we have a small, inconsequential reference to an old woman who has just died. She is portrayed coming down to earth, and being part of the real not fantasy world, where honesty and truth prevail, and hypocrisy is superseded. People going about their every day business are totally disinterested in an old deflated woman about to hit the ground.

OOP!

OOP is an acronym for the Opening of Parliament. *The International Comedy Awards 2003* exposes the comicality inherent in an outrageously hyped up ceremony of anachronistic imperious pomposity. This past its use-by-date Soap Opera is a derisory show staged each year in Britain. It highlights the conceit of Monarchy and any person who has the ignorance and temerity to be associated with it. Its existence exposes a nation's naivety. The irony being that those who watch it, witness more than 50% of elected MPs, swearing allegiance to a system of unelected tyranny that at times is **above the law** and therefore the very **antithesis of real democracy.**

I was unfortunate enough to see OOP on a United States TV news presentation, hence the reenactment here. My guests were amused but puzzled by the hilarious and embarrassing ritual. In their magnanimity however, they were generous enough to commiserate with my predicament and thereby ease my raging discomfort.

In the cartoon, the Queen accepts an award that reflects badly on her, other royals, the Monarchy and by marked association the nation. Regrettably our children are also involved, innocent victims of a peculiar and dire system that should be eradicated from their world. Prince Philip is portrayed as a buffoon who embarrassingly for Britain puts his foot in it again!

The Queen's Speech

The Opening of Parliament, **OOP** as seen in another cartoon is justifiably one of the most comical events in which two royals participate. However, the Queen's Speech takes top spot for the most boring non-event ever to appear on our national TV network. It was reported nationally that the viewing figures were in serious decline, down to just 3 million out of a population of over 50 million. To boost the viewing figures it was suggested that statisticians include pets in their future calculations. Whether it was said as a joke or not it makes for interesting reading! And yet on the front page of The Guardian 29-04-03, the BBC decided to drop Mastermind… "when ratings fell to 6 million"!!! Why then, does the BBC continue to torment and waste the time of the British public, and squander public money, by broadcasting a non-event like the Queen's speech? Published figures confirm that the ratings have fallen to 3 million, well below the ratings of Mastermind in 1997! Is someone engaged in Royal sycophancy here?

It will be interesting to see how the British Broadcasting Corporation reacts if viewing figures for the reintroduced programme Mastermind do not reach their anticipated levels of 6 million?

This cartoon is a reconstruction of that potential scenario. The room is packed with different types of bored animals. Only the cheese holding mouse is alert, wearing an expression of shock and disbelief, thinking perhaps, what a load of rubbish and give me a *Tom and Jerry* movie any day. A royal flunkey is feeding a soggy biscuit to an almost bored to death resident in some unnamed royal residence. Above him a sickly smiling Queen's mother looks down with obvious maternal pride. The British bulldog, symbol of a bored nation vents his disapproval.

Axis of Evil: Islamic Perspective

To give balance to the propaganda expounded against the Arab world by the West it is necessary and important that alternative viewpoints be considered. No matter how justified the reasons for war may appear the consequence is death and destruction, a fact that those in British society campaigning for peace will condemn without reservation. And yet Britain and the Monarchy will undoubtedly be involved in further conflict with Islam in the decades to come.

This cartoon highlights Islam's axis of evil, the three **Bs. Bush, Battenberg and Blair.** Bush is the gung-ho gun toting leader of the gang, Blair is in the supporting role, while Battenberg is menacing as she wields her iron mace in the background. Her attitude relates to the-oath-of-allegiance that the British military swear to the Queen, their Commander-in-Chief, and confirms the behind the scenes import of the Monarchy during times of conflict. A major thrust of this cartoon is to draw attention to the dangerous role that our Monarch plays in any aggression. A role which would minimize risk of a revenge attack against her or her relatives, if she revoked it. Revocation must take account of the oath-of-allegiance and the royal prerogative whereby a Monarch is undemocratically able to wage war without waiting for approval from the people of Britain. Relinquishing the oath would transfer responsibilities, risks and decisions of war making directly to **the British people,** who would then have a democratic **choice** of expressing their views and influence via the ballot box.

A right that at present is denied the British people by the tyranny and absolutism of Monarchy.

February 2004. Now that the legality of the Iraq war is being pursued through International Courts of Justice, will Queen Elizabeth the Second, as Commander-in-Chief of Britain's armed forces, be questioned about the leading role she played in the whole tragic affair, or will she be allowed to wallow in undemocratic privilege and be regarded as beyond the law of the land?

The Oath of Allegiance

The British military have no choice but to swear allegiance to the Queen. As a consequence she, and they, are in default of proper democracy. Furthermore, the nation is constantly reminded that it is Her Majesty's Army, Navy and Air Force, a doctrine that confirms how unrepresentative the people's oath-of-allegiance is. Allegiance should encompass its people first, then the nation. No individual should be given an honour that supersedes the legitimate electorate, an absolutism that we and hopefully the international community will encourage Britain to disown. Our unelected Monarch is Commander-in-Chief of all branches of the military, many of whom carry the pre-fix Royal. Consequently, it is irrational and improper for our Head-of-State to distance her or himself from the realities and politics of war. They cannot plead with hands held high that it has nothing to do with them. Should the oath-of-allegiance remain in its present form, they must stand the consequences of the committal, no matter how tragic the outcome. Until that day of change comes, every bullet, shell and bomb is sent to maim and kill in the Monarch's name.

This cartoon exemplifies that fact. Our unelected Monarch exerts enormous political influence, and being at the centre of government has the power to revoke the oath and royal prerogative which allows her as Head-of-State to make war in our name. The people of Britain including our highly proficient military should welcome such a gesture and mark it as a staging post towards <u>long awaited democracy and true citizenship.</u>

As a people's patriot, I would fight to the death for this country, protecting family, friends and people but never royalty or Monarchy. To uphold Monarchy is to deny Britain a true democracy. As a loyal people's patriot this would be seen as an unpardonable act of treachery and betrayal of millions of fellow loyalists who support the same democratic ideology and love of country.

Rodents Royal

Press reports have confirmed that bunkers in Royal establishments (paid for by the British taxpayer?) have been extensively refurbished to make them safe havens from chemical and biological attack. The bunkers, allegedly, contain the latest high-tech filtering equipment, specialist protective clothing, and ample quantities of food for a long siege. Also included allegedly, are state-of-the-art electronics, vast supplies of food, booze and huge quantities of un-named luxuries. The media have been prohibited from taking photographs, because the images could compromise security?!

Buckingham Palace is illustrated, but there are allegedly, **selected bolt-holes** throughout Britain for them to scurry to. The image of rodents correlates the analogy between a _sinking_ ship and a city and its people being deserted by the royal entourage. Two generations of royals are included to highlight the continuing tyranny and privilege of Monarchy. The eyes looking up show others have already occupied their places of safety. Outside the railings are **two children, terrified** by their isolation, exclusion and lack of protection. Children are used to symbolize the British nation, left fully exposed to an attack. For the royals to accept the bunkers for their own protection was an appalling misjudgment. It magnifies a privileged and self indulgent class intent on saving their own necks while **we and our children** are rendered helpless and exposed to the horrors of chemical and biological terrorism when it comes. Far better if they had refused the hideaways in the first place.

Which they could have done!

Royal Porton Down

Before royalty opens or gives its name to anything, exhaustive checks are made to eliminate any adverse and potentially damaging after effects. They open Bridges, Hospitals, Stadia, all structures that rest comfortably within their 'common subjects' psyche. Each event is hugely propagandist for the royals and Monarchy as well as politically motivated, although they would deny it. Royalty is encamped at the centre of British politics, but continues to offend the nation by trading on tyranny and denial, blocking our right to **elect** a Head-of-State. Royal Porton Down (my title), is a government establishment that was NOT opened by royalty, (although from 1916 to 1929, it temporarily carried the prefix Royal). No spin doctors, No fanfares, No hype, No Royal propaganda! Nevertheless, it is one of Her Majesty's research centres where civil servants and scientists work who swear an oath-of-allegiance to Britain's unelected Monarch. It may be argued that Porton Down exists to produce "anti-dotes" for use against the proliferation of chemicals and biological "poisons" being produced around the world, but why produce the poisons in the first place? Dangerous substances have been manufactured there; perhaps Ricin was one of them. If this is the case, who were the unfortunate person(s) or nations earmarked to receive them? Our "Holier-Than-Thou" attitude regarding OUR possession is sanitised for public consumption. How different when an undesirable country has control of them!! All hell breaks loose.

The illustrations and motive behind this cartoon go some way to debunking Britain's sanctimonious attitude. Unfortunately the hypocrisy displayed here is still rife in the British establishment and at the very heart of Monarchy. While the Royals are safe in their reinforced bunkers and able to cope effectively with any eventuality thrown at them, one message within the cartoon is loud and clear for the rest of us.

"Take cover under the stairs or wherever you can folks, our deadly concoctions are returning home with a vengeance!"

Autocracy Suzerainty Tyranny

In May 2003 a British TV network showed us the exercise books of schoolchildren in Iraq. The front cover of each featured the face of their elected Head-of-State Saddam Hussein. The propaganda was denigrated as a flagrant abuse of power, notorious and so on. A form of self-promotion to be despised and rejected and one more reason to justify the West's resolve to 'liberate' Iraq. And yet there was no mention, or comparison made between Saddam Hussein's face on exercise books and Iraqi banknotes and that of our unelected Head-of-State the Queen and her face on millions of British stamps and banknotes. In both examples the children of each country had no choice but to accept the imposition. What hypocrisy what cheek from the British establishment and media! The three words in the title are linked one way or another with the politics of Britain. As long as this ***septic*** isle of ours is encumbered with an unelected Head-of-State, we have no choice but to acknowledge each of the conditions conferred in the title. Our Monarch has absolute power in vital areas, and absolute control to some degree in a state that is internally autonomous. Tyranny on this occasion however, refers not to overt cruelty but the arbitrary and repressive covert power that is rooted in a lack of choice for the legitimate electorate. If this point is raised with Monarchists they predictably harp on about the tyranny of Stalin, Amin, Hitler or Saddam Hussein for example. Do you want a tyranny like that they ask? Of course not you dunderheads! The tyranny in Britain is subtle, low key and insidious, but extremely damaging to Britain nevertheless, and must be eradicated from our culture without delay.

As responsible parents, we should demand that our children be free from this deplorable subliminal, sinister, mistletoe tyranny sooner rather than later. *Enough is enough!!*

In this cartoon the facts are clearly explained, but regrettably yet again, the British media and establishment is gripped firmly by the politics of prejudice and misinformation. In this instance like so many issues involving the Monarchy and royals, we must ensure that our children are given a choice.

The Royal Chatelaine

The Queen's mother occupied a dominant role in British society. In particular her alleged position as chatelaine of royal misdemeanors which are, allegedly confined to the vaults at Windsor castle. An impenetrable fortress of royal secrets and monarchy shattering issues?? Information denied scrutiny by the British taxpaying public. A situation ensuring that a tarnished dysfunctional family and an institution built on deceit within hereditary privilege is able to conceal revelatory information that for the majority of us would probably be made public. The recent TV drama *The Lost Prince* was a splendid example of facts being sanitised in defense of royalty. Presumably someone in authority decided to continue the Queen's mother's philosophy of deluding the British public. If the events portrayed in the drama were factual, it is clear that the prince, far from being lost, was an unfortunate victim of abandonment and cruel child abuse. Is this yet another deferential whitewash and further instance of the British media being *ridiculously reverential* towards royalty?

Reference to her alleged obsession with betting, the bookies, and installation of her own private wire at Clarence House is touched on in the cartoon. Is this one more royal secret that our deferential press haughtily prevented the British public from knowing? If true, we need to know why British taxpayers money was wasted in this way. Especially when so many people are surviving at poverty levels on reduced benefit payments. Although only five cupboards are shown, it is reasonable to surmise that there are other cupboards and more secrets that could be openly aired. In the 21st century it is scandalous for the royals, who are kept by British taxpayers, to be able to continue to cower behind their high blown and privileged status.

Prince Oink!!

Hereditary privilege takes many forms, a lot of it hidden from public scrutiny. Prince Andrew, however, was recorded ranting and raging in full view of those present at the time of the incident. Two ordinary 'commoners', were selling fast food outside the gates of Buckingham Palace. Objecting to the aroma of cooked food, Prince Andrew resorted to **abusive behaviour** presumably to get them removed from the scene. Although they were allegedly, NOT in contravention of any bye-law. This man could so easily have retired to any one of the six hundred or more rooms available to him, but he seemed set on confrontation. It was an outrageous example of royalty exerting its privilege in a thoroughly bad and rude manner. Such **threatening behaviour** could be construed as disturbing the peace. And if committed on the public streets of London by anyone else would certainly have ensured police intervention. Should there ever be a next time, members of the taxpaying public would be entitled to respond in like manner or worse?

The cartoon records the situation. The railings have been partially removed to emphasize Prince Andrew's irrational and unwarranted response to an incident that eventually resulted in the vendor's license being revoked. The vendor outraged at the ranting behaviour, expresses the views of the majority by throwing a punch at the royal snout. In fact the fast food supplier showed remarkable constraint and declined to get involved in such yobbish behaviour.

I offer my sincere apologies to the species of animal used as a model.

'Herr' Battenberg?

The poor and unfortunate **immigrants** desperate for aid and comfort in Britain and the rest of Europe are seldom out of the news these days. A variety of checks and demoralizing interrogations are implemented. Was this the case with Philip Battenberg, our German or is it Greek settler when he came to live in Britain? Did he experience and suffer the same indignity? It is clear that his recent ancestors, Alice of Battenberg, Andrew of Greece and before that Louis of Battenberg and Victoria of Hesse did not exclude him from investigation. Whatever the reason for his acceptance by the British establishment, it would be interesting to read the documents relating to his application, if they exist. If not, then why not?

The cartoon highlights the hypocrisy in the British establishment and suggests that this man should have sought a tax paying job, thereby exempting him from state handouts. Furthermore, it is demoralizing for the rest of us to see someone acceding to the awful degrading royal protocol set before him.

February 2004. Ah now we have it, immigrants wishing to settle in Britain can become 'citizens', as long as they swear allegiance to our unelected Queen. In Britain however they are not absolute citizens as in the exceedingly democratic countries of France and Germany for example, but 'Citizen' SUBJECTS. The whole ceremony, attended by a government Minister and Prince Charles was a farcical and mocking attempt at progressive democracy and a terrible deception perpetrated against not only the immigrants but the rest of our cosmopolitan nation also.

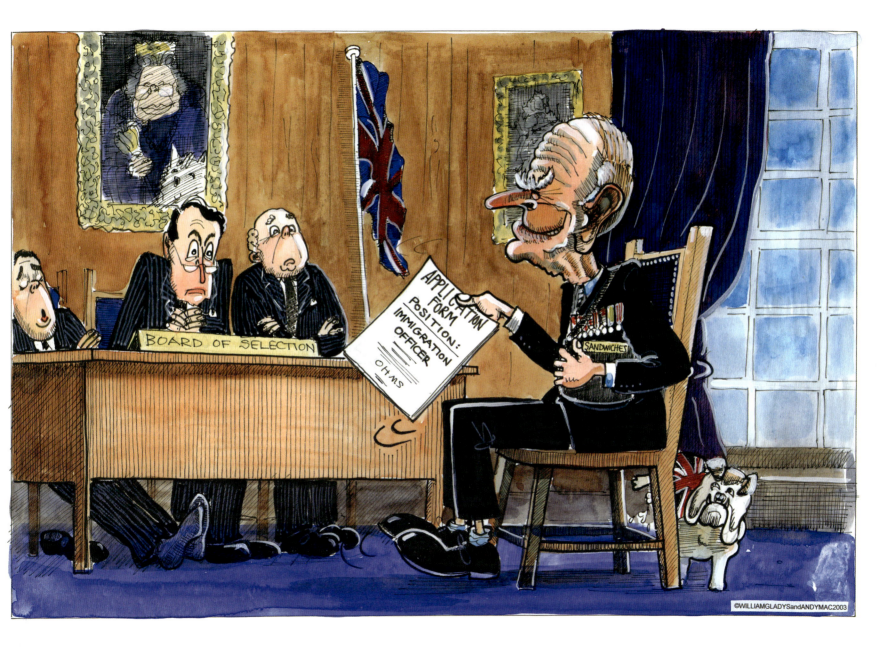

Royals State Benefits Increased!

It is public knowledge that Charles, William and Harry, are to receive enormous benefits from the British taxpayer when they move into Clarence House. Camilla and her father will be tagging along. This huge property was refurbished at a cost in excess of £4 million! Why wasn't Prince Charles asked to settle the bills from his annual income of £7 million or William providing funds from his mother's inheritance? Why is Camilla allegedly being paid a **weekly 'pittance' of £3,000 from public funds?** Moreover, will she and her father be contributing to the upkeep and maintenance of the property, assuming that they are both very wealthy individuals in their own right? Wouldn't it be prudent for us to know what *their* financial status is as they appear to be profiting from state benefits also? None of these questions would come about normally, but the British taxpayer is handing over huge sums of money to a privileged few who, it could be argued, can well afford to finance improvements themselves. Knowledge that two rooms will be decorated and paid for by Camilla and her father is a red-herring surely? Are they not going to use the other rooms so lavishly redecorated at the taxpayers' expense?

In the cartoon we see three of the royals being driven to Clarence House with Camilla and her father in the boot accompanied by jewels and a couple of crowns thrown in for good measure. To the left is one of the many waste bins full of taxpayers' money being emptied, with our hard earned cash disappearing like magic in the wind? **The Daily Guff** expounds its usual stuff to gullible British readers taken in by the deplorable spin. On the **Daily News** poster, a widower and his two children are recorded waiting months and months for their rightful taxpaid benefits. Similar examples are common but without knowing the exact figure, could there be in excess of half a million hard up people waiting for their benefits to arrive? Meanwhile, a pampered and privileged minority goes to the front of the queue and lives it up in style at the publics' expense?

TIME FOR CHANGE.

Grovelling Subjects

Sycophantic grovelling of children towards royalty is considered praiseworthy and encouraged by certain elements in the right wing British press. An article in 2003 highlights the disreputable and subversive aspect of this in our media. Obviously, some parents and some teachers are also guilty of acquiescence to royalty on this issue. How sad that they unthinkingly and with apparent pride nonchalantly deny British children their absolute right to lawful democratic citizenship!! A concurrence that unfortunately condemns our children to remain servile and deferential subjects. (The recent introduction of an oath for immigrants refers to citizens, but this is a misnomer and will remain so until the Monarchy and its allusion to a person as a 'subject' remains). This non-action positively ensures that the next generation will unconsciously position themselves as inferior people in thrall to an institution that is class divisive, practices religious discrimination and is based on an unelected tyranny that is self perpetuating.

An irresponsible example for our children to follow!

In the cartoon we witness Britain's unelected Head-of-State as she sits in one of her six hundred plus rooms at Buckingham Palace. Two of her many flunkies wait in trepidation as she absorbs the sickening contents of a letter from her schoolchildren subjects. If she possesses a modicum of sensitivity and is able to soak up the toe-curling <u>cringe factor</u>, she will soon be puking into the receptacle provided.

Queen Elizabeth's Faux Pas

The Queen accompanied by her husband purportedly committed a social blunder of the highest order! Refusing to eat the spaghetti or pasta dish so carefully and fastidiously prepared for her by her Italian hosts was an exceptionally ungracious and rude act. Let us trust that people of other countries will not have to suffer similar insults and disrespect in the future, and that the British nation be protected from further insensitive acts of humiliation by our unelected Head-of-State.

In this cartoon, the incident is recalled, with The Queen turning her nose regally upwards and forcefully declaring: "Bring me what he is having", while pointing at the bangers or frankfurters and mash that her husband is consuming with gusto. Inclusion of bangers or frankfurters and mash is relevant. It reminds the reader of the correlation that exists between the Queen's common behaviour, that of a common but enjoyable dish and her recent Germanic ancestral lineage.

<u>Bad behaviour should always be condemned unequivocally. Why should anyone be expected to tolerate it because it issues from a Head-of-State?</u>

Written Constitution? DENIED!!

It is an outrageous imposition on the people of Britain to be denied their lawful right to a written constitution. Each and every one of us should be empowered with a guarantee that no individual is above the law.
The cosmopolitan people of our nation can only attain this assurance of equality and liberty through legislation. While Monarchy remains however any hope of achieving this and so much more will be **denied** us. We will remain **stigmatised** as servile subjects not confident citizens. It is a stigma that many powerful individuals and committees still condone however and are prepared to accept. A recent example on TV illustrates just one way in which this is achieved.

The live inauguration speech of President Bush was relayed to Britain uncut by some TV networks. He praised the citizens of America, and stressed that they were no longer subjects. In edited British versions broadcast later, the word subjects had been deleted!! Yet again we witness the power and influence of Monarchy on an unsuspecting and gullible British public and another example of toadying to royals? Whether you admire the present President of the U.S.A. or indeed his policies, the facts are that he is the most powerful person in the world, and lives in and defends a Republic. There are many checks in place to ensure that he does not exceed his power. The President cannot go to war without the approval of Congress. In Britain the undemocratic royal prerogative and absolutism prevails. As subjects not citizens we have no choice. The unelected Monarch in Britain however has the power to make **WAR!** without consulting the people. Not an ideal democracy is it?

The cartoon shows a sweating <u>subject</u>, the PM being dominated by our unelected Head-of-State. Papers seven and twelve have been shelved. Item seven relates to the previous mêlée to exclude the Queen's head on postage stamps and give people the choice to decide. DENIED! Item twelve refers to a long overdue written constitution. While any PM resorts to weekly audiences at Buckingham Palace, what likelihood is there of major reform being discussed openly? This is not to imply that anything remiss has occurred, but doubt and suspicion will always remain in the minds of our nation's people. If only for that reason, these bizarre influential and high-handed meetings should be rescinded.

Ethics of Royal Cleansing

At the trial of Paul Burrell the royal butler, serious allegations of rape at St. James's Palace were published in the British media. It was acknowledged that there would be a thorough In-house investigation of the alleged criminal behaviour at the behest of Prince Charles and a senior advisor. An In-house perquisition can never be considered the correct means to uncover truths behind such serious accusations however. It seems odd therefore, that the British police have decided (allegedly) not to investigate the matter further. This approach is inconsistent with similar allegations of 'celebrity' misconduct. The British public has a right to know the truth. Whether they get it is another question, and yet it is our money that is contributing to the royals extravagant and highly suspect lifestyle. What is going on? Is there one law for royalty and hereditary privilege and a different one for the rest of us? Indeed, with the intervention of our unelected Head-of-State in a recent court case it looks as if there is a two tier system in place in "democratic" Britain. Does anyone seriously believe that this blatant example of interference in Britain's judicial system should not be legislated against? The whole business still needs investigating. Is everything really in the open? Why is the media allowing its readers to be fobbed off in this manner? The grubby palace carpet must be removed and given a thorough external cleaning. The British taxpayer should not be satisfied with a cheap in-situ shampoo!

This cartoon is a reenactment of the investigation. Prince Charles is doing a wonderful promised clean up. He wields the In-house broom vigorously ensuring that everything is spick and span and squeaky clean on the surface. All will soon be revealed for the British public's consumption. Looking through the proffered crack in the curtains however, a public servant, a policeman, peers with a single eye, acting like a bounteous but neutered Cyclops, surveying all but seeing nothing!

Princely Hypocrisy

The nation is frequently being urged to buy British by Prince Charles, and yet he orders a German Audi car for his own use!! Ja Audi Ich Dien! No one takes him to task over his hypocrisy. No one asks for a face-to-face interview and explanation. Too many times the British public is encouraged to swallow his outbursts as the gospel according to Prince Charles. It will not do, and should not be tolerated. His political involvement over GM crops is a prime example. He is entitled to make his views known, but must not hide behind his privileged position when challenging questions are put to him. He issues a statement to the media; the media publishes it, but does not push for a one-to-one discussion or a public meeting with those who hold opposing views. This is royalty cashing in on their undemocratic position of privilege.

Prince Charles, either debate matters in public or shut up.

The cartoon shows him driving his Teutonic purchase. The number plate carries the Prince of Wales motto Ich Dien. How very true!! Whether the German models are manufactured in Britain or not is an irrelevance. This immensely wealthy royal should have purchased a proven **British** marques Rover or Jaguar instead.

Moreover, he could have had the **British** car sprayed in its historical colour of British Racing Green. This would have matched his incessant political letter writing to the PM in green ink!!

What hypocrisy. What privilege. What cheek!!

Royals Don't Trade? Ha Ha!!

For centuries the nation has been encouraged to follow the "myth" that trade is beneath royals. This sarcastic, snobbish phrase 'in trade' only referring to non-royals! Have these lack brains never heard of a King's ransom where a life was traded for gold, or the 'adventurers', better described as pirates, sent to plunder and trade in the name of the Monarch? An extension of this blinkered, silly and prejudicial belief still exists today! "Royals are above trade". What tripe. The majority of them willingly trade their titles for the publicity and propaganda it gives them. Distinctive examples are the Coat of Arms advertised on buildings, and on numerous goods traded for the public to purchase. We also have the Queen's Awards to industry, a good example of this woman trading her title for a product she probably knows little about or ever seen. How esteemed if a product had been endorsed by an expert in the trade or profession or a highly popular celebrity instead.

Added to the trade myth is yet another equally absurd fancy that, "you never mention a toilet seat when speaking about the Queen"! Reaffirmed yet again on British TV in 2003. What foolish priggish nonsense!! Let us puncture such pompous preciosity and snobbery forthwith!!

All royals urinate, defecate, sit on toilet seats, use toilet paper, break wind, belch, blow their noses, and change their underwear!

The nonsensical fancy referred to is a sound reason for including Prince Charles. Biologically, all royals are the same as us. To have a person with a ridiculous fairyland title selling mundane toilet rolls, with his lover helping out in the back of the 'Charlie boy' van, and Prince Philip doing a right royal job shows them in a real down to earth concept. Encourage the media to scorn the deferential titles, Prince, Duke and H.R.H. and position this appalling clique in their proper place in society, as Citizens of Britain. To eliminate criticism in the future, royals should stop benefiting from their titles, whether it be Coat of Arms, Awards to industry or the trading in organic or other goods from their homes,(where it is hoped planning permission has been sought.) In the detailed illustration, this grasping dynasty is shown trading commercially and politically. The cartoon evolved from this type of continuous, insidious, subliminal, covert royal propaganda. Of major concern to everybody is that they do so at a significant advantage to the rest of us.

Finally, none of the royals have a divine right to rule. Trash that nonsense before it becomes a myth!

Ja Ich Dien

It is common knowledge that Prince Charles writes ream upon ream to government departments and the Prime Minister. His letters are oddly, written in green ink, and the contents denied public examination. Whether we are given access to them or not, it is clear that the prince is heavily engaged in promoting his political objectives. And by association includes the Monarchy as well. No longer can the Monarchy be labelled apolitical! The time is right therefore, for the people of Britain to harvest the royals and Monarchy into an elective republic. No more deceit, no more delusion, no more hiding behind privilege, no more insidious political manoeuvering. At last he will be able to enter the real world and be part of a people's government. Join us as Citizens, no longer subservient subjects in thrall to your mother! Well done Charles Battenberg, as you will now be known. You have disowned hereditary privilege, rejected tyranny and obstructive denials; you have given the country a lead in the right direction. Well done!!!

Well the nation can dream!

The Royals will never give up power politics voluntarily; we have to continue the fight to get rid of them by all legitimate means available to us. Although ironically their power and influence has ensured that any protests or objections cannot now be held outside Buckingham Palace. Certainly a rule and favour too far!! The cartoon encapsulates the political campaigning of Prince Charles. Will his envelopes and letters emblazoned with the **garish** Prince of Wales feathers and crest be relegated to the bottom of the in-tray and dealt with in polite chronological order? Draw your own conclusions until we hear to the contrary! The major thrust of the cartoon is to remind people that his mother is our unelected Head-of-State. Does his privileged status allow him to gain political advantage over the rest of us? How many policy changes has her government made as a result of his incessant writings? His mother has the ear of our elected Prime Minister. It is not unreasonable to expect that Prince Charles is reaping the benefit of that relationship? An unelected Head-of-State, or any royal for that matter, must not be allowed to curry favour on any issue that gives royalty an unfair political advantage over the legitimate electorate of Britain.

Harry Shaven Head?

In some press reports we are informed that 'evil' people are anxious to get hold of a strand of Prince Harry's hair. It would be more apt to describe them as People Detectives anxious to seek out the 'truth' and not willing to be fobbed off with misleading information tossed to them, by royal spin-doctors. Obviously some group is interested in exploring the facts about Prince Harry's paternity. It is alleged that his father is not Prince Charles. In the years to come facial development will probably settle the matter for us anyway. In the meantime, why not resolve the matter in a dignified manner by offering a few strands for independent analysis? Invasion of privacy is not paramount when an allegation of such magnitude and possible deceit of a nation is under investigation. Sadly, whatever the final scenario, Britain will be internationally embarrassed and humiliated yet again by royalty and Monarchy!!

The cartoon shows an army of royal servants and machinery at full throttle being used to prevent any residuum from falling into the 'evil clutches' of the nation's People Detectives.

Shifting the Goalposts

About a decade ago, the media denigrated corporate fat cats who were paid astronomical salaries. And yet one of the fattest cats, the Queen, was outlandishly exempted from scrutiny and criticism. No public searching questions were asked about our unelected Monarch's exclusion from paying tax for decades, and certainly no apologies given to the British tax paying people, although a modicum of time was allocated in parliament. Apparently special tax arrangements for her are fair and justified. Hogwash!! On a tour to the U.S.A. some years past, paid for by the British public, they pleaded poverty. Now a British newspaper informs us that this woman's fortune has reached a staggering eleven hundred and fifty million pounds! To make matters worse, we learn that no inheritance tax will be paid on her mother's estate. An "estimated" loss to this nation of ours of about £20-million! A special arrangement to exclude the Queen from inheritance tax is yet another insult to British taxpayers, who by their own diligence have earned and saved enough to benefit their children when they die. The brutal truth however is shocking:

When WE die inheritance tax will ensure that OUR children will not get their entitled inheritance!

This cartoon shows two of the royal fat cats feeding off British society. One of her grandsons is included because he will presumably be benefiting from her tax shenanigans at a later date. The begging caps in the foreground include the Chancellor of the Exchequer, whose training expertise and hard work appear unrewarded in comparison to our un-elected Head-of-State. As for the rest of us: Rail workers, Firemen, Nurses, Teachers, other Public employees, centuries of taxpayers, the hardworking worthies? They must of course go cap in hand to get THEIR rightful dues. Not so the royal fat cats, who no matter what always get the cream! Incidentally, where has all that untaxed income for the Queen gone? All public expenditure should be transparent and accountable.

We all have a right to know where <u>our money</u> has been put.

Royal Bloo Blud

For centuries Britain has been fed the nonsensical myth of blue blooded aristocracy. The aims of the myth makers, is to position the rest of us in a psychologically deferential and subservient role to royalty and the old aristocracy. The term 'blue blooded' is class divisive, insulting, anachronistic and snobbish. An abhorrent monster imposed surreptitiously on the people of Britain and which should be removed from our gullible nation's terminology – *except in comic form when it relates to aristocracy* – as soon as possible. In the Oxford English Dictionary, Blue Blood is described as follows.

Belonging by. . . birth to the aristocracy.
Having fine personal qualities or high moral principles.
Imposing, magnificent.

Well surely after all the continuing scandals we have had to suffer over the years, clear thinking people will conclude that items two and three can be excluded from the royal equation!! The two examples are better qualified to describe the great numbers of 'commoners' in Britain who are not recipients of mythical blue-blooded rubbish but have the admirable red type running through their veins.

In this cartoon the absurd myth of Blue-Blood is placed in a correct and sane perspective. The three royals illustrated have given samples of their blood to a nurse whose mind, subjected to a relentless bombardment of royal subliminal misinformation all her life, exclaims with shock and surprise. It's Red! To one side we see a sample box with the results grouped as O Negative, the commonest type of blood. Not blue at all! Of course we do not (yet) know their blood groups, but it will be 'researched' and published one day in the public interest. Until that day we have to speculate that royal blood types are predominately O Negative. The same as Fred in the fish market. Oh How Frightfully Common!

Backward Britain

The possible coronation of Prince Charles, or any other royal, will expose a garish, antiquated and preposterous ceremony that has no relevance in the 21st century. At the present time however the royal establishment appears hell-bent on renewing such nonsense, ignorant of world-wide amusement, embarrassment and damage that it would cause to Britain's image. It is mind boggling to think that in the new millennium, when space exploration is commonplace, nano science is breaking new frontiers, <u>people</u> democracies are being encouraged for other countries, that Britain concentrates much of its energies on anachronistic royalty, Monarchy and coronation!!

Here we see an embarrassing enactment of the proposed coronation of Prince Charles. The cartoon is based on a published tape in which the clown prince is heard talking to his lover about tampons. His stupidity is emphasised by a crown of tampons and shared hilariously by the younger generation who have been reminded of the joke. The next generation, symbolised by the choir in the abbey and not fed mis-information on royalty and Monarchy, like previous generations, are no longer in step with the absurd establishment organised circus that befronts them.

Princely Silence

It is ironic that while his mother's military is waging war against Islam, Prince Charles is ingratiating himself with children who follow the same faith: Islam. And yet no matter what aspirations our children may have, each and every one of them will be denied their democratic right to become Head-of-State. The tyranny of royal hereditary birth and royal undemocratic prerogative ensures this. Confirmation that Britain is controlled by absolutism and a long way from an ideal of a people's democracy. It is outrageous that in the 21st century, our children are forced to adulate members of a dynasty who are maintained by state handouts and wallow in hereditary privilege. Certainly not a healthy ideal for parents and teachers to set before the children of Britain.

In the cartoon we see Prince Charles dressed inappropriately in his passé suit and tie as he addresses schoolchildren in a run down multi-faith school. The seated boy is bored. In the waste bin are discarded propaganda leaflets distributed by Monarchical sycophants. To hand are numerous costly minders paid for by the British taxpayer, and protecting him from face-to-face criticism and protest as he campaigns for political support from the socially and religiously disadvantaged. The thought bubble reiterates the double think and hypocrisy so rampant within the royal life style.

Buck Palace People's Park

A modern progressive people's architect put forward the idea that railings surrounding Buckingham Palace be removed, the gardens given to the people, and the palace façade improved. To add to this we suggest the palace be converted and opened up for daily public use. Importantly admission should be free, unlike at present where the entrance fee to a small part of the building is expensive. An irony being that the British taxpayer contributes £millions towards its upkeep and then has to suffer the double indignity of paying again to gain access!!

This cartoon was in response to the architect's patriotic and feasible ideas. The theme park illustrated is an extreme one but could work, although unlikely to be approved! However, there are many uses that the grounds and building could be used to benefit everyone rather than a privileged few. Leisure areas in London are at a premium so this would be an ideal site to alleviate a major problem for the people in the city. As for the rather odd people employed in degrading and deferential jobs, no doubt these could be found satisfying and worthwhile employment elsewhere. The Queen with an estimated fortune of £1500 million has ample finances to compensate each one. Likewise there is adequate property available to house her and her hubby, Windsor, Balmoral or Sandringham for example. It may be that the nation will confiscate one or more of the remaining properties later. To retain more than one for a privileged family is uneconomic and immoral while there are so many people in Britain in need of decent accommodation.

The Queen's Mimicry

Balmoral estate is huge. If the information given me is correct, it covers about 16,000 acres of Britain's national heritage. The estate was allegedly the subject of grant aid for fencing, a large sum of money probably provided by the British tax paying public. Do not forget that this woman is one of the richest in the world!!! A point that beggars the question why did she not pay for the improvements from her own fortune? Furthermore, why was she so intolerant of an innocent family simply wanting a miniscule share in her good fortune, and which they had almost certainly contributed towards?

The cartoon derives from unpleasant mimicry that she allegedly made to the media about a family of her subjects who inadvertently trespassed through an open gate onto a small area of the estate. Such irate and ungracious behaviour is recorded here. Her attitude, apart from being indecorous and mean, was thoroughly objectionable. Her ingratitude towards those in our unequal society who are less privileged is not to be tolerated. After all, it is this sort of family who at present, and unwisely, are contributing towards her privileged and luxurious lifestyle. Quadruple shame on you ma'am. An apology is due. Perhaps her son, who is keen on rural issues, will campaign for fairer rights of access to the countryside for the **taxpaying British public.** In particular the huge estates that most of us would like to enjoy for rambling, picnicking etc. but which at present are only available to his mother and other members of their clique to use for their own solitary and selfish pleasure.

Royal Train: "Frightfully Good Value"??

Well now we know! The cost of the Royal train extravaganza is a loss to Britain of only sixty pence per person. Put in explicit terms £872, 000, for a few trips in a single year. Extremely costly and wasteful and certainly not "frightfully good value" *for us* as our billionaire Monarch would have us believe. The keeper of the quaintly named Privy Purse "dictatorially" informs the taxpaying public that it will probably stay for another fifteen years! To rub salt in the wound we learn that any **right to object will be denied us**. This arrogant impromptu remark commits the people of Britain to further profligate expenditure on our unelected Monarch. Thirteen million pounds at least, plus maintenance (not itemised in the statistics). One reason given for continuing these lavish trips is the age of both royals, 77 and 82 years respectively. Well tell that to the millions of pensioners who can ill afford even a small luxury on their pitiful state pension, let alone champagne and first-class trips on trains. While the British people suffer interminable delays at mainline stations, how many timetables have been re-scheduled to accommodate this royal nonsense? The royal life style is wayward, un-warranted and un-sustainable. Taxpayers' money must not be wasted in this way. It is time for this rail relic of the Imperial past to be sold and exhibited for a paying public to visit. Only then will it begin to earn its keep and help recompense the people of this country after years of frivolous unjustified expenditure. Moreover, the people will want questions answered once they see first hand the colossal luxury and waste that was involved.

This cartoon states that it was not "frightfully good value" for her 'commoner' subjects. Nevertheless there are still oddities out there that are prepared to acquiesce to the outrageous and grovel before it! Mr. and Mrs. Utterly-Servile and their two children cringingly demean themselves by bowing and curtseying as the royal couple and their extravaganza hurtles by. (Do not forget that in the 21st century, this 'time capsule' woman still expects women and children to curtsey before her!!) What impudence. What nerve! The Queen and her husband are witnessed living it up (at our expense), as they disdainfully pass just two of our nation's deprived old age pensioners, who, averse to acknowledging the extensive royal frippery raise their fists and umbrella in anger.

Royals Rocket Orff to Mars!

Should the British people ever be fortunate enough to witness this event, 'people democrats' would be celebrating. Millions of people yearn for Britain to throw off the yoke of feudalism, tyranny and denial, all present in the anachronistic institution of Monarchy. There is a growing realization that Monarchy (and those responsible for it) are the 'enemy within' holding generation after generation in thrall to servility and deference as subjects, denying them true citizenship. It is time to free our children from this dreadful imposition once and forever. At present they have no choice but to bear allegiance to royals and Monarchy and remain subjects all their lives. The previous cartoons have shown how damaging to Britain Monarchy and royals have been. Our children, without realizing it, are force fed this soul destroying nonsense from the time they learn to speak. First the dreary National Anthem. The melody and lyrics drummed into them from day one should be superseded without delay. It is wholly unrepresentative of the people, focusing instead on an unelected Head-of-State, who occupies an exalted position not by worth but hereditary birth. A shocking piece of propaganda to set before our children. (The people of Scotland and Wales have already rejected it!) Secondly, we have the embarrassing and internationally humiliating titles of Queen, Prince, Duke, Duchess, HRH etc. to contend with. Each one designed to put our children in an appropriate lowly and demeaning position. HRH is not only silly, but insulting. What is your child in comparison to a Highness? Lowness!! Parents, teachers, how derisory can it get? Why are you forcing your children to be conditioned in this way and making them accept such an undignified demeaning and dissolute position in the world? They deserve so much better.

The cartoon simply reiterates all that has been said above. However, although a rocket is used as a means of eradicating this scourge from British society, there are obviously other ways in which it could be achieved and illustrated!!
(The company names and logos used on the side of the rocket are purely imaginary)

Absurd ceremonial Flag Flying Days in Britain

In the 21st century Britain is still encouraging its gullible and innocent children to celebrate hereditary privilege and the damaging exultation of Royal mediocrity, Here is a list taken from a current (21st century!!) flag sellers catalogue of Royals we are sadly forcing our children to adulate. February 6th Accession of the Queen… February 19th Birthday of Prince Andrew… March 10th Birthday of Prince Edward… April 21st Birthday Queen Elizabeth… June 2nd Anniversary of Coronation… June, Queen's official birthday… June 10th Birthday of Duke of Edinburgh… June 10th Birthday of Prince William… August 15th Birthday of Princess Anne… September 15th Birthday of Prince Harry… November 20th Anniversary of Queen's wedding.

Children! What deception & piffle for you to swallow!

Here is a new list for parents and teachers to put before their children, although there are many other people of excellence that I have left out due to lack of space. Let our children emulate and celebrate brilliance and leave dull and restrictive mediocrity behind. Newton, Darwin, Churchill, Keats, Brunel, Jane Austin, Virginia Woolf, Britten, Dylan Thomas, Aneurin Bevin, Lloyd George, Professors (Female and Male) of Medicine, Science, Music, Engineering, History, Politics, Architecture, Astrology, Psychiatry, Psychology, Literature & Arts, Criminology and etc. from Scottish, Welsh and English Universities, (Lords of the second chamber excluded, judged as feudal and class divisive), Fox Talbot, Great British inventors, bright stars in the Entertainment sphere. These are the people we should be asking our children to emulate. Let us start today. Vote for twelve each year and fly the appropriate flag once a month in celebration of their greatness. (The honours list is derisory, and prejudiced because it allows our unelected Head-of-State to promote her political agenda MUK Monarchy UK. in perpetuity. Something to be deplored and rejected in the interest of an improved and better British democracy in the 21st century)